101 Games, Drills and Exercises for Future Black Belts

FL Allman

Copyright © 2018 by FL Allman

All rights reserved.

No portion of this book may be reproduced in any form without written permission from the publisher or author, except as permitted by U.S. copyright law.

Contents

Disclaimer	IX
1. A Quick Note About Terminology	1
2. Prologue	2
3. EASY WARM-UPS	4
4. Lucy	5
5. Tony	7
6. Sam	9
7. Meet Me In The Middle	11
8. Pick a Card	13
9. WAYS TO USE YOUR BELT	17
10. The Ali Shuffle	18
11. The Ali Shuffle Jab	19
12. Belt Jump Lunges	20
13. Belts!	21

14. Tails	23
15. Windmills	24
16. Under / Over Side Kicks	25
17. Belt Thief	26
18. Bonus Belt Thief	27
19. Trapeze Push-Ups	28
20. Trapeze Squat Thrusts	29
21. Chariots	30
22. Snake Pull	31
23. Sitting Pull	32
24. Egg Slicer	33
25. KICK PAD DRILLS	35
26. Hard or Fast	36
27. Ap or Yop	37
28. Pyramids	39
29. Run!	41
30. Robots	43
31. The Kicking Beep Test	45
32. Saved By The Bell	47
33. Follow Me	49
34. Pest	51
35. 21	52
36. KICK PADS AREN'T JUST FOR	54

KICKING

37.	Pass The Pad	55
38.	Throw and Spin	56
39.	Shield Pivots	57
40.	Shield Slams	58
41.	Shield Throws	59
42.	Dodge Pad	60
43.	Doctors and Spies	61
44.	Chaos Kicks	63
45.	Flying Side Kicks	64
46.	HITTING CHILDREN WITH STICKS?	65
47.	Duck & Jump	66
48.	Dodge & Double Dodge	68
49.	Combos	69
50.	The Whacky Game	70
51.	Bubble Blaster	72
52.	Blocker Party	73
53.	Buzzy Bees	74
54.	Magic Wands	75
55.	Blocker Tag	76
56.	Blocking Tag	77
57.	SPARRING GAMES	78
58.	Shoulder Tag Sparring	79

59. Butt Kicker Sparring	81
60. Roundhouse Tag	82
61. Extreme Roundhouse Tag	83
62. Strip Sparring	84
63. KATA DRILLS	86
64. Memory Kata	87
65. Mirror Kata	89
66. Kata in a Box	90
67. Remote Control Kata	91
68. Applied Kata	93
69. TAG YOU'RE IT	95
70. Toilet Tag	96
71. Zombie Tag	97
72. Crazy Crawling Zombies	98
73. Stuck in the Side Kick	99
74. Jailhouse Tag	100
75. Dollyo Tag	102
76. Ninja, Ninja, Turtle	104
77. Quiet Ninjas	105
78. Budge	106
79. Kicks Vs Punches	107
80. BODYWEIGHT DRILLS	108
81. Superman Bananas	109

82. Bottom Balance Wars	110
83. Sumo Balance Wars	111
84. Plank Balance Wars	112
85. Tunnels	113
86. Roll Over	114
87. King Of The Mats	115
88. Crab Sparring	117
89. Helicopters	119
90. Burpee Ladder	120
91. TAEKWONDO: THE MUSICAL	121
92. Ghostbusters	122
93. Sally	123
94. Cups	125
95. Cha Cha Slide	126
96. Three Lions	128
97. HAPPY HOLIDAYS	130
98. The 12 Days of Kickmas	131
99. Advent Calendar	133
100. Last Class Of The Year	135
101. First Class of the Year	136
102. The Nice List & The Naughty List	137
103. 10 MORE GAMES	139
104. The Ninjas Are Coming	140

105. The Opposite Game	142
106. Creeping Lions	144
107. General Choi Went to the Dojo	146
108. Higher or Lower	148
109. Prove It	149
110. Taekwondo Master	151
111. The Shuffle Game	152
112. Ninja Jumps	153
113. Ninja Statues	154
114. THE FINAL FAVOURITE - DRILL 101	155
115. Bully It, Save It	156
SO LONG, FAREWELL	158

DISCLAIMER

By using any ideas in this book you assume all risks associated with teaching or coaching martial arts. It is the reader's responsibility to ensure they are fully qualified, insured, and have undergone a criminal records check to work with children and vulnerable adults. It is the reader's responsibility to carryout risk assessments prior to delivering a new training exercise or game.

A Quick Note About Terminology

I come from a taekwondo background but to keep things simple I've used non-taekwondo terms where more widely recognisable ones are available.

Therefore:

I've used *dojo* instead of *dojang*.

I've used *round kick* instead of *turning kick*.

I've used *kata* instead of *tul* or *poomse*.

Prologue

'If your students are bored and uninterested, it's because you're being boring and uninteresting!'

Allow me to tell you a little about myself and my martial arts journey. I promise not to ramble on too long.

I suppose I'm a career martial artist. At the age of seven, I remember asking where Dad disappeared to every Monday and Thursday. He told me about the taekwondo classes he was attending so I started to go along with him, not to join in, just to give Mum some peace and quiet. I would sit at the back of the hall colouring in or playing with my toys. After a while, there was a group of us kids just hanging around at the taekwondo club. We'd chat and cause trouble until the instructor decided to start a junior class in the hopes of tiring us out. I haven't really looked back.

I competed in local and national tournaments from the age of ten and after passing my black belt exam at sixteen I made it on to the national team and began to travel internationally for tournaments. Whilst I was thoroughly addicted to taekwondo and could think about and talk about nothing else I had no idea that I would become an instructor myself. I attended university and gained a first class honours degree in Sport and Exercise Development and although most of my classmates planned on becoming personal trainers, I wanted to crossover into English or media studies and become a sports journalist.

In the days after my final university exams the local leisure centre had undergone a refurbishment and was advertising for sports instructors. I thought 'I have a black belt, I've attended an instructors course, I need some money...'

So I started my first taekwondo class and it sold out in less than 24 hours. Word began to spread and more and more local parents wanted their children to train with me, so I opened a second class, and a third, and a fourth and before I knew it I'd stopped looking for a nine to five job and realised that I was now living the dream; my hobby was paying the bills.

Almost fifteen years later and my hobby is still paying the bills. Whilst I teach all age ranges my real joy is teaching children and watching them grow from shy, nervous white belts into strong, confident black belts. I have put together this collection of my favourite drills, games, and exercises to help fellow instructors have as much fun in their classes as I do in mine. My classes are taekwondo based but these drills will cross over into karate, kickboxing, and other martial arts.

Here's to not being boring and uninteresting.

EASY WARM-UPS

Lucy

Age range: All ages.

Goal: Raise the heart rate, mobilise joints, allow students to contribute to the class.

Named after one of our black belts, this warm-up is super simple and gets members of the group involved in shaping the warm-up.

Have the group line up across one side of the hall.

Everyone runs back and forth across the hall until they have completed five shuttles.

Call the name of a student. That student shouts out a technique. i.e. Rising block.

Everyone in the group performs ten rising blocks.

The group complete another five shuttles and wait for the next student to be called.

Continue for as many sets as you like. We usually do up to eight sets.

Option - Use exercises instead of techniques to include a little more fitness. Star jumps, burpees etc all work well in this warm-up.

When selecting which student will pick the next technique, I choose someone who tried really hard on the previous one. They don't have to be the best, they just have to show me that they tried.

TONY

Age range: All ages.

Goal: Raise the heart rate, mobilise joints, allow students to contribute to the class.

Named after another of our black belts, the Tony involves a lot of shuttle runs.

Get into pairs and set a timer for around eight minutes. (Set a longer or shorter time depending on the age and fitness levels of the group).

Student A goes first. He shouts an exercise to Student B, i.e. Push-ups. Then he begins his shuttle runs.

Student B performs push-ups until Student A has completed five shuttle runs.

Student B shouts an exercise for Student A to perform while she starts her shuttles.

Complete as many sets as you can in the time allowed. You'll find the exercises become harder and harder and students try to get their own back on their partner for the previous exercise choice!

Adults' classes: We sometimes use dumbbells in our adults' classes and this exercise works nicely.

SAM

Age range: +8.

Goal: Raise the heart rate, increase upper body strength and endurance.

You guessed it. Named after one of our black belts. Sam loves push-ups so there are plenty in this warm-up. You'll need a partner, a kick pad and a set of gloves.

After completing five push-ups, grab your pad and perform fifty punches each.

In each round the number of push-ups and punches stays the same but the style of push-up varies.

In total, you do fifty push-ups and five hundred punches!

Rounds:

- Normal push-ups.

- Wide push-ups (twice shoulder width).
- Narrow push-ups (hands in a diamond formation).
- Scorpion push-ups (lift one leg as you lower down).
- Spiderman push-ups (pull one knee to the side of the body as you lower down).
- Decline push-ups (rest your feet on an elevated surface such as a bench or a kick shield).
- Tiger push-ups (switch between the high and low plank).
- Butt kicker push-ups (after each push-up, kick your heels up to hit your bottom).
- Push-up and side hold (after each push-up, rotate onto one hand and hold a side plank for five seconds).
- Slow motion push-ups.

Too easy? In an advanced or older classes you can increase the numbers to ten push-ups and one hundred punches per set. Black belts might even go for twenty push-ups per set.

Too hard? If you want this drill to go faster, have everyone perform the punches as shadow work rather than using pads.

MEET ME IN THE MIDDLE

Age range: All ages.

Goal: Raise the heart rate, mobilise joints, promote teamwork and timing.

Stand facing your partner at opposite ends of the training hall. During each round you will run to the centre of the hall to meet your partner then return to where you started three times.

In round one, run to the centre, meet your partner and high-5 with the right hand. Run back to where you started and perform one star jump. Repeat this but do two star jumps. Then, repeat a final time with three start jumps.

When all the teams have finished, move to round two...

Rounds:

- Round one. Right high-5.

- Round two. Right high-5, left high-5.
- Round three. Right high-5, left high-5, right 'foot-5', left 'foot-5'.
- Round four. Right high-5, left high-5, right 'foot-5', left 'foot-5', turn back to back and high-5 above the head then through the legs.
- Round five. Add on two high-5s from the plank.
- Round six. Add on two sit-up high-5s.
- Round seven. Add on a burpee high-5.

Thats twenty-one shuttles, forty-two star jumps and loads of coordination.

Pick a Card

Age range: All ages.

Goal: Raise the heart rate, mobilise joints, promote fun and variety.

For this warm-up you can either use a physical set of playing cards or you can download an app that randomly generates one each time you tap the screen.

Set a timer for five to eight minutes and have each student choose a card. When they have completed the corresponding exercise they choose another.

Continue until the time runs out.

Hearts:

1. 1 push-up
2. 20 punches
3. 3 push-ups
4. 40 punches

5. 5 push-ups
6. 60 punches
7. 7 push-ups
8. 80 punches
9. 9 push-ups
10. 100 punches

Jack: 50 uppercuts

Queen: 75 uppercuts

King: 100 uppercuts

Diamonds:

1. 1 lap of the hall
2. 20 round kicks
3. 3 laps of the hall
4. 40 round kicks
5. 5 laps of the hall
6. 60 round kicks
7. 7 laps of the hall
8. 80 round kicks
9. 9 laps of the hall
10. 100 round kicks

Jack: 25 star jumps

Queen: 50 star jumps

King: 75 star jumps

Spades:

1. 1-minute plank
2. 2-minute wall sit
3. 3 burpees
4. 40 front kicks
5. 5 burpees
6. 60 front kicks
7. 7 burpees
8. 80 front kicks
9. 9 burpees
10. 100 front kicks

Jack: 50 mountain climbers

Queen: 75 mountain climbers

King: 100 mountain climbers

Clubs:

1. 1 burpee with push-up and tuck jump
2. 2 jumping kicks
3. 3 burpees with push-up and tuck jump
4. 4 jumping kicks
5. 5 burpees with push-up and tuck jump
6. 6 jumping kicks
7. 7 burpees with push-ups and tuck jump

8. 8 jumping kicks
9. 9 burpees with push-ups and tuck jump
10. 10 jumping kicks

Jack: 50 high knees

Queen: 100 high knees

King: 150 high knees

WAYS TO USE YOUR BELT

A martial arts belt is a great tool for warm-up exercises, conditioning games, and drills. Here are a few of ways we use belts as training aids in our dojo.

The Ali Shuffle

Age range: All ages.

Goal: Improve footwork and coordination.

Named after the late, great Muhammad Ali. The Ali Shuffle involves quickly changing stance from orthodox to southpaw and back again.

Lay your belt on the floor and stand with one foot in front of the belt and one foot behind it.

Bring your arms up into a guard.

Switch your stance as quickly as you can for fifty to one hundred repetitions.

Optionally, you can give penalties for landing on the belt. A couple of tuck jumps will do.

The Ali Shuffle Jab

Age range: All ages.

Goal: Improve footwork and coordination. Teach the difference between a jab and a cross.

This is just like the last drill but instead of just switching stance, your students need to perform a jab on each switch.

This drill is not only great for fitness and coordination but it is also a useful tool for teaching the difference between southpaw and orthodox and teaching that the jab is always thrown from the lead hand, regardless of which stance you are in.

Option 1 - Add in a penalty for touching the belt.

Option 2 - Add in a penalty for dropping your guard.

Progression - Change jabs to crosses and use the rear hand each time.

Belt Jump Lunges

Age range: +8.

Goal: Improve leg strength and coordination.

With your belt on the floor, stand with one foot in front of it and bring your hands into a guard.

Lower your rear knee in a lunge so that your knee almost touches the floor.

Jump up and switch stances, landing back in a lunge position.

A set of twenty should help to tire out the thigh muscles.

Option - Add in a jab or cross on each lunge.

Progression - Do this exercise facing a partner and keep time with them.

Belts!

Age range: All ages.

Goal: Just for fun.

This is one of our absolute favourite games. The adults class love it as much as the juniors.

Have everyone take off their belts and scatter them around the dojo.

Everyone runs about in the hall in a large circle. You could also have your students skip, shadow spar, crawl. Whatever you like.

The instructor closes their eyes and shouts 'BELTS!'

Everyone grabs the nearest belt and holds it in the air.

The instructor (still with their eyes closed) shouts a colour. i.e. 'Black belt!' Anyone holding a black belt has to do ten burpees or five tuck jumps, whatever you choose.

Option - Swap the rules around and give penalties to anyone NOT holding that colour belt."

TAILS

Age range: All ages.

Goal: Improve footwork (dodging), spatial awareness.

Everyone removes their belt, folds it in half or thirds and tucks the end into the back of their trousers. Now everyone has a tail.

On the command 'GO!', everyone runs around the hall and tries to steal the tails from other players.

If you steal someone's tail, throw it to the edge of the dojo and carry on playing. If you lose your tail, run to the edge of the dojo and complete ten star jumps before tucking your tail back in.

WINDMILLS

Student A is kicking and punching. Student B holds the kick shield. Student C stands to the side of the kick shield and swings their belt round and round in a windmill fashion so that the length of the belt passes in front of the kick shield.

Student C should try to maintain a steady rhythm.

Student A needs to time their kicks and punches so that they don't get caught by the belt.

Beginner students might only fit in a single technique between belt swings. More advanced students should be able to do three or four move combinations.

Under / Over Side Kicks

Age range: All ages.

Goal: Increase leg strength and flexibility.

Student A folds their belt into thirds and stands in front of Student B.

Student A should hold their belt horizontally in both hands, with about 40cm between their hands. Their arms should be stretched forward so the belt isn't too close to their body.

Student B chambers for a side kick and performs a set of ten kicks without putting their foot on the floor. Each kick should alternate between passing under the belt and over the belt.

Progression - Start at hip height for beginners and progress to head height to black belts.

Belt Thief

Age range: All ages.

Goal: Just for fun. Improve sprint speed.

Have your students remove their belts and place them in a pile in the centre of the dojo. Split your students into four teams and have each team take a corner of the room.

Students take turns running the to the centre, grabbing a belt and taking it back to their team.

Only one person from each team can run at a time and you can only pick up one belt at a time.

Continue until all the belts have gone. Which team got the most belts? The winning team gathers all the belts back to the centre for the next game while the other teams complete ten burpees.

Option - Black belts are worth two points.

Bonus Belt Thief

Age range: All ages.

Goal: Just for fun. Improve sprint speed.

In this version of the game, once all the belts have gone from the centre of the hall, the game continues with students taking belts from other teams.

Teams can not guard their stash. Continue until the instructor yells 'TIME!'.

Which team has the most belts?

TRAPEZE PUSH-UPS

Age range: +10.

Goal: Improve core and upper body strength.

In pairs, have one student adopt a plank position. Their partner loops a belt under their ankles to lift their feet off the floor about six inches.

From this position you can make push-ups a lot more demanding. This drill is best for older stronger children who can easily manage ten or more chest to floor push-ups.

Trapeze Squat Thrusts

Age range: +10.

Goal: Improve core and upper body strength.

In pairs, have one student adopts a plank position. Their partner loops a belt under their ankles to lift their feet off the floor. From this position the person in the plank position can pull their knees in and out to their chest. This makes squat thrusts a lot more demanding on the core and is also a great arm workout for the person holding the belt.

Tip - stand to the side of the person doing the exercise rather than behind them.

Chariots

Age range: +10.

Goal: Strength and endurance.

Have your students get into pairs and stand at one end of the dojo. One student stands behind the other, wraps a belt around their partner's middle and takes hold of the ends. The student in front has to run to the other end of the dojo while their partner holds on and tries to slow them down.

SNAKE PULL

Age range: +10.

Goal: Improve upper body strength.

My students love this exercise but they need to be partnered up with someone of similar weight. This also works best on a wooden floor rather than on mats.

Student A lies on their belly and holds the end of a belt in their hands.

Student B sits at the other end of the belt. They grip it tightly and anchor their feet into the floor.

Student A pulls themselves along the belt using only their arm strength. (Keep those feet off the floor!)

When they reach their partner, Student B scurries backwards, plants their feet again and the pair continue until they reach the end of the dojo.

SITTING PULL

Age range: +10.

Goal: Improve upper body strength.

This is just like the previous drill but instead of lying on your belly, sit on your bottom and lift your feet off your floor.

If your balance is off you will spin around onto your back. The exercise still works from this position. Just pull the belt above your head.

Egg Slicer

Age range: -8.

Goal: Improve timing. Duck and jump skills.

This is a fun exercise for your younger students, however, it can be a little dangerous if students are being silly, so save this game for your better-behaved classes.

Have your students stand in the middle of the dojo.

Tie three or four belts together and have two assistants hold the ends and spread the belt over the width of the dojo.

The assistants run from one end of the dojo to the other keeping the belt on the floor so students have to jump in time to allow the belt to pass from one end of the hall to the other.

You can also lift the belt up to head height so that your students have to duck at the right time to let the belt pass to the other end of the hall.

KICK PAD DRILLS

Hard or Fast

Age range: All ages.

Goal: Teamwork, boxing technique, speed and power development.

Students get into pairs and move around the dojo.

Student A should have their guard up and be light on their feet. Student B raises the pad to head height and either shouts 'HARD' or 'FAST'.

HARD = perform two hard punches.

FAST = perform four fast punches.

Instructors should be able to hear the difference in speed and power.

Option - Change punches for round kicks. HARD = a single hard kick, FAST = a double kick.

AP OR YOP

Age range: All ages.

Goal: Teamwork, kicking technique, speed and power development, learning terminology.

In a lot of taekwondo clubs, students are encouraged, or required, to learn the Korean terms for the various techniques they practice. We use this drill as a way of helping youngsters learn some of the basics.

Students get into pairs and move around the dojo.

Student A should have their guard up and be light on their feet.

Student B holds the pad for a side kick or front pushing kick. They shout 'AP' or 'YOP'.

AP = '*Ap cha milgi*'. Perform a front pushing kick.

YOP = 'Yop cha jirugi'. Perform a side kick.

Progression - Hold the pad for a round kick. Shout 'Dollyo' for a turning kick (AKA round kick) or 'Bandae' for a spin kick. Use whichever terms are relevant for your style.

Pyramids

Age range: All ages.

Goal: Teamwork, kicking technique, speed and endurance development.

A classic. Put your students in pairs and have them stand at opposite ends of the dojo.

Student A runs to their partner and performs a single side kick before running back to where they started.

Student A returns to the pad but this time they perform two side kicks.

Repeat with a set of three, then a set of four... You get the idea.

If you continue up to ten the student will have performed fifty-five kicks.

This drill works with a huge range of kicks and strikes.

Run!

Age range: All ages.

Goal: Teamwork, boxing technique, speed, and endurance.

Pair your students up at one end of the dojo and choose a simple technique. For this example, we'll use punches.

Student A holds the pad head height and Student B starts punching as fast as they can. (Keep those guards high!) Emphasis on speed, not power.

When the instructor yells 'RUN!' all the punchers must run to the other end of the hall as fast as they can. As soon as they return they continue punching.

Young children - Little ones have a habit of running into their parter when they return from the shuttle run. To prevent this, I ask them to perform a burpee before they can start punching again.

You can mix it up by shouting 'RUN!' when the students aren't quite back to their partners so they have to turn and run again.

You can also be a bit silly and shout words that sound like *run* to try to catch the students off guard. I use *ruuuunny eggs*, or *ruuudolf the red nose reindeer*.

Continue until everyone's arms are thoroughly tired out, then swap the teams over.

Robots

Age range: -8.

Goal: Teamwork, technique, memory skills.

This is a fun exercise for younger students. Divide your group into threes. Student A will be the robot. Student B will hold the kick shield. Student C controls the robot.

Student C stands behind the robot and taps them on either the arm or leg.

If student A feels a tap on their right arm, they perform a right punch. If they feel a tap on their left leg they perform a left kick.

Give each student a minute to be the robot.

In the second round, students double up the commands for the robot. They might feel a tap on the right arm then the left arm. (Right punch, left punch)

Or, they might feel a tap on the left leg and the right arm. (Left kick, right punch)

In round three try three commands.

The Kicking Beep Test

Age range: +10.

Goal: Kicking technique, endurance, timing.

Most people are familiar with the beep test. If you aren't, it involves running back and forth over a fifteen or twenty-metre track in time with a series of beeps that get faster and faster.

At our club we made a kicking version of the beep test. You'll need an interval timer and a speaker.

There are five rounds of twenty kicks. One hundred in total.

Round 1: The beep sounds every five seconds. Perform a back kick after every beep.

Round 2: The beep sounds every four seconds. Perform a side kick after every beep.

Round 3: The beep sounds every three seconds. Perform a hook kick after every beep.

Round 4: The beep sounds every two seconds. Perform a round kick after every beep.

Round 5: The beep sounds every second. Perform a front kick after every beep.

Progression - Try this drill but all kicks are jumping.

Saved By The Bell

Age range: +8.

Goal: Technique repetition, speed, endurance, timing, and teamwork.

Set your interval timer to beep every seven seconds for forty reps.

Choose a five move combination. For this example we'll choose; Jab, cross, hook, double side kick.

Student A holds the pad in the correct position. Student B gets into a guard.

On the bell, Student B performs jab, cross, hook, double side kick, then takes the pad ready for Student A.

Each student has only seven seconds to perform the combination and get the pad ready for their partner's turn.

Each student should perform twenty sets each.

Too easy? Choose a six move combination or add in kicks that require more time such as jumping or spinning kicks.

Follow Me

Age range: All ages.

Goal: Distance control, teamwork, endurance.

This drill tires out the arms and is useful for gauging distance and movement.

In pairs, have Student A hold a focus pad. Student A can move left and right along a straight line.

Student B has to continuously punch, meaning they need to read their partner's movements so that they can stay in front of the focus pad.

Start slowly and get faster and faster.

Option 1 - Instead of moving left and right, have Student A move forwards and backwards. This really puts emphasis on distance control. 'Long arms. No baby punches!'

Option 2 - Student A pivots on the spot. Student B has to move around in a circle to stay in front of them.

Pest

Age range: +10.

Goal: Distance control, teamwork, power development, footwork skills.

Get into pairs and grab a kick shield.

Student A is being a pest! They continuously follow Student B, trying to get as close to them as possible.

Student B holds the pest at bay with push kicks, side kicks, back kicks and good footwork.

21

Age range: +10.

Goal: Perseverance, endurance, technique repetition.

Time to bring some basic math into the dojo!

Choose two simple techniques. For this example, we'll use punches and side kicks.

Everything has to add up to twenty-one. So, in the first round you'll perform twenty punches and one side kick.

In the second round you'll perform nineteen punches and two side kicks.

In the third round you'll perform eighteen punches and three side kicks... You get the idea.

By the end, you will have performed two hundred and ten punches and two hundred and ten side kicks.

Option - If this takes too long or is too difficult, drop it down to ten.

KICK PADS AREN'T JUST FOR KICKING

We use two main types of pads in our club; big heavy kick shields and small 'smartie' pads. There are many ways to use these items for conditioning or playing games and they don't always involve kicking and punching.

Pass The Pad

Age range: All ages.

Goal: Just for fun.

Again, this is a martial arts version of a children's party game.

Sit your students in a circle and hand out a few focus pads. When the music plays the students pass the pads around the circle. If the music stops while you are holding a pad you need to do twenty mountain climbers.

Option - reverse the game so anyone not holding a kick pad gets mountain climbers.

THROW AND SPIN

Age range: All ages.

Goal: Teamwork, coordination, honesty.

In pairs, stand three - four metres away from each other. Using a chest pass, pass the kick shield back and forth between you.

After throwing the kick shield you need to jump in the air and spin 360° in time to catch the shield as it's returned to you.

Dropped the kick shield? You and your partner have to do five burpees.

Shield Pivots

Age range: All ages.

Goal: Core strength.

Sit on your bottom and lift your feet off the floor so that only your bottom is touching the floor. Hold the kick shield in both hands and bounce it back and forth from the right side of your body to the left. This is a great way to build core strength and can be used as part of a circuit or in team races. Try ten to one hundred reps at a time, depending on the age and ability of your group.

SHIELD SLAMS

Age range: All ages.

Goal: Upper body strength, just for fun.

My students love this exercise because it's so noisy!

In teams, have the first student in each queue run down the dojo, carrying a kick shield. At the end of the hall, they slam it as hard as they can onto the ground. It should make a loud bang. They run back and hand (not throw) the shield to the next person. The team with the loudest slams can choose a penalty for the other teams.

Simple but fun.

Shield Throws

Age range: All ages.

Goal: Upper body strength.

Have your students form queues at one end of the dojo. The first person in each group picks up their kick shield and throws it as far across the dojo as they can. They then run forward, collect the shield and hand it to the next person in the team. Make sure they don't throw the shields back. You can add in a little competition by placing a cone where the best throws have landed.

Dodge Pad

Age range: All ages.

Goal: Teamwork, spatial awareness, coordination.

Divide your class into two teams and place a bench or a line of belts across the centre of the hall to create two playing areas.

Use focus pads as dodgeballs (no head shots). If you hit a player on the other team they are out and sit at the edge of the hall.

Continue until one team runs out of players.

Doctors and Spies

Age range: All ages.

Goal: Teamwork, spatial awareness, coordination. Tactics.

This is a progression from the previous drill.

For this version of the game have each team secretly choose one team member to be *The Doctor*.

If a player is hit, instead of moving to the side, they lie down on the floor. *The Doctor* can run over and bring them back to life by touching them on the shoulder.

Be careful! If *The Doctor* is hit, no one can bring him back into the game.

Option - Each team chooses a player to be *The Spy*.

If *The Spy* has the pad they are allowed to run over the dividing line to take their shot.

Be careful! The Spy is only allowed in enemy territory for five seconds at a time and they will be an easier target when they are over the line.

Chaos Kicks

Age range: +8.

Goal: Spatial awareness, coordination.

Everyone in the class grabs a small focus pad and holds it over their stomach with both hands. You are not allowed to move your pad from your stomach.

On the instructor's command, everyone runs around the room trying to kick other player's pads whilst not being kicked on their own.

Students should be reminded to use control and adjust the amount of power in their kicks for smaller members of the group.

Option - If someone kicks your pad, run the edge of the dojo and do three burpees before playing again.

Flying Side Kicks

Age range: +8.

Goal: Technique repetition, lower body power development, balance.

I have a few students who are obsessed with this exercise and want to do it at the end of every lesson.

Use your kick shields as hurdles to practice jumping kicks. My juniors love testing themselves with jumping kicks, especially flying side kicks. Sometimes we pile the kick shields on top of each other to make a super high hurdle. One of my students can clear a pile of eight!

Option - Instead of piling the shields up, space them out so students can jump for distance instead of height. Either way, it's a lot of fun.

HITTING CHILDREN WITH STICKS?

OK, so technically we aren't hitting children with sticks... We're teaching them defensive skills using blockers... But that's not as much fun to say.

What is a blocker? A blocker is a tool used by instructors to teach blocking without ending up black and blue from bruises. It is usually a plastic stick covered in sponge with a small amount of stick left uncovered to act as a handle. You can use improvised blockers as well, we prefer to use thick pipe insulation cut into 1m lengths but I've seen other clubs using swimming noodles.

Duck & Jump

Age range: All ages.

Goal: Spatial awareness, coordination, footwork skills.

Hand out blockers to your assistants and divide your class into teams. The person at the front of the team runs forward and gets into their guard. The assistant swings the blocker towards the student's head and they duck in time to avoid it. They should bend from the knees rather than bending over to look at the floor. Encourage the students to keep a good guard as they do so.

Next, the blocker swings in towards the student's feet and they jump in time to avoid it. Again, encourage students to land with a good guard.

Option 1 - Change the order randomly. Sometimes do duck then jump, sometimes jump then duck.

Option 2 - Have the assistants hold a focus pad in their free hands. After each duck or jump, the students can strike the pad with a counter attack.

Dodge & Double Dodge

Age range: All ages.

Goal: Spatial awareness, coordination, footwork skills.

The first student in the queue should run forward and get into their guard. The assistant swings the blocker straight down like an axe. The student should jump to the side to dodge out of the way.

Progress on to the double dodge. Dodge to one side on the first swing and get back to the other side before the axe swings again. Be careful not to dodge too far on the first swing, as you won't have time to get back to the other side.

Option - Add in counter-attacks.

Combos

Age range: All ages.

Goal: Spatial awareness, coordination, reaction speed, memory skills.

Here's where it gets fun. Combine duck, jump and dodge with various blocks and you can make any number of sequences to practice.

Here are some of my favourites:

- Duck, jump, dodge, dodge, rising block.
- Right head block, left head block, duck, counter.
- Jump, jump, round kick, jab, cross, duck.

THE WHACKY GAME

Age range: +8.

Goal: Just for fun. Sprint speed, control, spatial awareness.

I used to call this game 'Lying Down Blocker Tag,' but my students renamed it and it's sort of stuck now.

Have everyone lie face down in a space and tell them that they can not move unless they are being attacked.

Give an assistant a blocker and have them start hitting one student on the back with it (the age of your students and type of blocker you use will determine how hard or soft you can go for safety).

The student who is being hit (Student A) jumps to their feet and runs away, the assistant chases them, still trying to hit them with the blocker. Note, you must run around the people lying on the floor and not jump over them.

To escape, Student A should lie down next to another student (B), now the assistant will go after Student B instead.

We play this game in my adult's classes too, but it gets a wee bit more violent!

Option - You can have more than one attacker playing at any one time, just use more blockers.

Bubble Blaster

Age range: -8.

Goal: Spatial awareness, coordination.

Hand out the blockers to your students and assign them a mat each to stand on so they can't run about and accidentally hit each other. Have your assistants walk about blowing party bubbles. Your students have to use the blockers to stop the bubbles from landing on the mats. You can also play this without blockers and have your students kick and punch the bubbles (it's harder than you'd think).

BLOCKER PARTY

Age range: +10.

Goal: Spatial awareness, coordination. Dodging and blocking skills. Control.

Blocker Party is a little bit chaotic but it's good fun if you have students who can be trusted not to get carried away.

The first rule is: No head shots!

Throw the blockers around the room and yell 'Go!' Everyone tries to grab a blocker and then run after their classmates, hitting them on the legs etc.

If you haven't got a blocker and you'd like to steal one, all you have to do is grab ahold of one. If someone grabs your blocker you must let go immediately.

Buzzy Bees

Age range: -8.

Goal: Spatial awareness, coordination. Just for fun.

Hand out a selection of blockers to your students. These are the stingers and should be held behind your students' backs.

The bees should run and spin around trying to tag their training buddies.

If you sting someone you lose your stinger and drop it on the floor for another student to pick up.

Magic Wands

Age range: All ages.

Goal: Spatial awareness, coordination. Lower body strength and endurance.

Choose a student or two, name them Harry, Ron, or Hermione (there's always one student who wants to be Voldemort) and give them a blocker but call it a magic wand. When the game begins your young witch or wizard will run around tagging their training buddies on the legs. If you are touched by the magic wand you turn into a frog and must bounce around performing 'tree frog jumps' (squat jumps) until the entire class has been turned into frogs.

Frog noises are encouraged!

Option - Have an assistant who has the antidote! If you frog jump over to the assistant they can high-5 you and make you human again.

Blocker Tag

Age range: All ages.

Goal: Control, spatial awareness, coordination, footwork skills.

Now it gets really silly! Hand out two or three blockers and explain that head shots are not allowed, only body shots.

Your students run about trying to hit as many people as they can with the blocker sticks.

Every time you are hit by a blocker, move to the side of the hall and perform a penalty before joining back in. Two tuck jumps will do.

BLOCKING TAG

Age range: All ages.

Goal: Control, spatial awareness, coordination, footwork skills. Blocking skills.

This is a continuation of Blocker Tag. This time we want to encourage some blocking and defensive work instead of just dodging.

It no longer counts if you are hit on the arms, so try to do some blocking rather than just running away.

SPARRING GAMES

Sparring doesn't have to be serious work all the time. There are many games and drills you can include in your practice as warm-ups and cool-downs or just to add a little fun and excitement. Here are five of our favourites.

SHOULDER TAG SPARRING

Age range: +8.

Goal: Reaction speed, accuracy, footwork.

This can be played with or without sparring kit. Pair your students up and after they bow and high-5 they begin to move as if sparring. Guards held high and footwork light.

Try to tag your partner on the shoulder whilst they try to do the same to you. You can dodge, block and feint.

If you are hit on the shoulder, be honest, stop and do a push-up before continuing the game.

Option 1 - TUMMY TAG SPARRING - Instead of tagging your partner's shoulder, tag them on the tummy. If you are hit do a sit-up.

Option 2 - THIGH TAG SPARRING - Try to tag your partner on the thigh using your foot. Round kicks and hook kicks are best for this game. If you are hit perform a squat jump.

Option 3 - TOE TAG SPARRING - Move like sparring but try to trap your partner's foot under your own foot. If you are caught, run a lap of the dojo before continuing.

Butt Kicker Sparring

Age range: +8.

Goal: Reaction speed, accuracy, footwork.

This is a silly way to warm-up for regular sparring and is less intimidating for those who don't like contact.

Move like sparring but you can only kick your partner on their bottom! There's always one kid who backs himself up to the wall... 'Ha! You can't get me!' But otherwise, it's fast, fun and promotes a lot of stance changes.

Roundhouse Tag

Age range: +8.

Goal: Technique repetition. Reaction speed, accuracy, footwork.

For this drill, put your sparring kit on and find a partner. Bow and begin to spar using round kicks only.

They can be low, middle or high, front or back leg, but that's it.

This is a simple drill but it really makes you focus on switching stances, staying light on your feet and working on your lift and shift technique.

Option - Take turns. Students have to wait their turn to kick. This makes the exercise more of a one-for-one sparring or kick-for-kick scenario and is easier for those who are new to sparring.

Extreme Roundhouse Tag

Age range: +8.

Goal: Technique repetition. Reaction speed, accuracy, footwork.

Similar to the previous drill, however different versions of round kicks are allowed. Switch kicks, double round kicks, jumping round kicks and 360s (AKA tornado kicks) can all be included.

Strip Sparring

Age range: +8.

Goal: Just for fun. Accuracy.

This drill is a good way to cool down after rounds of normal sparring training.

Everyone finds a partner, bows and touches gloves before beginning to spar.

If you score a point the round is over.

If you scored the point with a left punch, run to your kit bag (being aware of other people sparring) and put your left glove away.

Find a new partner and start sparring, but now you can't use your left hand.

If you score a right side kick, the round is over and you tidy your right foot pad away.

Find a new partner and continue (without any right kicks now) until you have lost both gloves and both foot pads.

At this point you are finished and can tidy away your head guard, shin pads, mouth guards etc.

Children who are finished should sit to the side and coach those who are still playing.

KATA DRILLS

Memory Kata

Age range: All ages.

Goal: Technique repetition, teamwork, memory skills.

Put your students into teams of three or four. Each team has to come up with their own kata and display it to the rest of the group. They only have ten minutes to practice.

Student A should pick the starting position.

Student B chooses the first technique, let's say a walking stance low block.

Everyone practices moving from the ready position to the low block three times.

Student C chooses the second technique (walking stance back fist strike).

Everyone practices moving from the ready position to the low block to the back fist strike three times.

Continue to take turns adding techniques to the kata until the time runs out.

Mirror Kata

Age range: +8.

Goal: Technique repetition, teamwork, concentration.

Pair your students into twos and have them select a kata that both members of their team know well.

One student will perform the pattern as normal and the other student will stand opposite them, performing the kata as a mirror image.

This is good fun and really tests you mentally, especially with the asymmetrical katas. Most of us build up muscle memory from years of kata practice and it takes a lot of concentration to overrule this muscle memory.

KATA IN A BOX

Age range: All ages.

Goal: Technique repetition. Just for fun.

This is a fun way to finish your kata practice. After running through a kata a number of times, tell your students to perform it once more but this time as if they are trapped in a phone box.

In other words, you can not move from your space. If you use square jigsaw mats you can assign each student a mat that they can not step out of.

Jump from one move to the next, switching stance instead of stepping forwards. Try to encourage students to still have good technique.

Remote Control Kata

Age range: +8.

Goal: Technique repetition, coaching skills. Just for fun.

Students choose a partner and select a kata to practice.

One student performs the kata as normal. (If they reach the end of the kata they can either start again or move onto a new kata.)

Their partner holds the 'invisible kata remote control' (I'm sure you can come up with a much cooler sounding name than that) and shouts commands to the other student.

PAUSE = Freeze. Here the partner can offer corrections to stances, body posture etc.

FAST FORWARD = Perform the pattern twice as fast as normal.

REWIND = Perform the pattern backwards.

PLAY = Perform the pattern as normal.

Applied Kata

Age range: +10.

Goal: Technique repetition, understanding technique applications, teamwork, memory skills.

In groups, one student will perform a kata, her teammates will be the attackers and defenders of each technique.

Let's use taekwondo pattern Chon Ji as the example.

The first move is a left low block. As the student turns to her left and performs the low block another student will execute a front snap kick for her block.

The second move is a right middle punch. As she steps forward to punch, her teammate will have to step back and block the punch.

These moves then repeat on the other side where another student will be waiting to execute a front snap kick and block her punch.

Continue practicing until the group has come up with attacks and defences to go with each move of the kata. You can have the groups display their work to the rest of the class.

TAG YOU'RE IT

Some of my classes are obsessed with playing tag. I'm not sure how many times I've used the phrase 'it's taekwondo club, not *tag*kwon-do club,' but it's a lot. That being said, we have hundreds of versions that we play during warm-ups or between exercises.

TOILET TAG

Age range: All ages.

Goal: Just for fun. Spatial awareness.

Who doesn't love a bit of toilet humour? This game works like stuck in the mud. Choose a student to be 'it', if they catch you, you turn into a toilet!

Crouch down and extend your arm to the side, this is your flush.

To rejoin the game you need to be flushed by another student. (Flushing noises encouraged!)

ZOMBIE TAG

Age range: All ages.

Goal: Just for fun. Spatial awareness and teamwork.

Everyone knows the best zombie films are the ones where the zombies can't run, they can only amble around slowly.

Choose a couple of students to be it. They can not run, only walk, arms extended, groaning like the undead.

Everyone else runs away. If you are caught, you become a zombie too. Continue until everyone in the class is a zombie.

CRAZY CRAWLING ZOMBIES

Age range: All ages.

Goal: Just for fun. Spatial awareness. Fitness and core strength.

This game has a similar concept but the zombies can move as fast as they like as long as they are on all fours.

Everyone else runs away as normal, if caught, they drop to their knees and join the zombie army.

Stuck in the Side Kick

Age range: All ages.

Goal: Just for fun. Spatial awareness. Fitness and leg strength.

Who want's to play stuck in the mud when you can play stuck in the side kick? For this game choose one or two students to be it, they chase the rest of the group and anyone who is caught must freeze holding a side kick.

To save someone and bring them back into the game you need to run under their kicking leg.

JAILHOUSE TAG

Age range: All ages.

Goal: Just for fun. Spatial awareness. Fitness and teamwork.

Pair your students up and assign an area of the dojo to be the jail. We use the back wall.

One pair of students will be the cops and the rest of the students will be the robbers. You don't need to stick with your partner but you must remember who your partner in crime is.

If you are caught by a cop, you go straight to jail. Only your partner in crime can free you from jail by running over and giving you a high-5.

Be careful! If you are caught by a cop before you can save your partner in crime you will both be stuck in the jail for the remainder of the game.

Play for rounds of one minute or continue until everyone is in jail.

Dollyo Tag

Age range: All ages.

Goal: Just for fun. Spatial awareness. Fitness and technique repetition.

Dollyo is the Korean terminology used in taekwondo for turning kick (round kick). As you can probably guess, this game involves round kicks.

Choose a couple of students to be it. They run about and catch their classmates by kicking their thighs with round kicks. (In a controlled manner, of course!)

If caught, you freeze and cross your arms over your chest.

To save a classmate, run to them and kick their arms with a round kick (again, with control).

Low kicks catch you and high kicks save you. This game teaches control and promotes flexibility as the smaller members of the group will need to kick high to save their taller friends.

Ninja, Ninja, Turtle

Age range: -8.

Goal: Just for fun. Reaction speed. Fitness.

This is the classic game of duck, duck, goose but with a ninja spin.

Everyone sits in a large circle. One student moves around the outside of the circle tapping each teammate on the head and saying 'ninja' as he does so. If he says 'turtle' as he taps your head, jump up and chase him around the circle.

If he gets back to your space and sits down before you can catch him, he is safe and you take over his role. However, if you catch him, quickly change direction, run the other way and try to get back to your space before you are caught.

Quiet Ninjas

Age range: All ages.

Goal: Just for fun. Reaction speed. Sprint speed.

Pair your students up and have them name themselves A and B.

A faces the wall and closes her eyes.

Student B starts at the opposite end of the dojo and creeps up on her as quietly as he can. When he is close enough B taps A on the back.

As soon as A feels the tap on her back she opens her eyes and chases B back across the room.

If B makes it the wall without being caught he wins and A does 5 push-ups. If A catches B before he makes it to the wall, he has to do the push-ups.

BUDGE

Age range: +8.

Goal: Just for fun. Spatial awareness. Sprint speed.

Scatter your kick shields around the room. You need fewer kick shields than there are players.

Each kick shield is a den where you are safe from being caught, however, only one student can stand on a den at a time.

If you are being chased and you want a den you must touch the person who is on den and shout 'BUDGE!' The other player must leave the den immediately and can not come back to the same den until they have been on another one.

Option - A more polite version is to change 'BUDGE!' to 'EXCUSE ME'.

Kicks Vs Punches

Age range: All ages.

Goal: Reaction speed, sprint speed, learning terminology.

Have students form pairs and line up in the centre of the hall facing each other. There should be around one to two metres between pairs depending on how fast your students are.

Take you place at the front of the dojo and explain that everyone on your right is 'team kick' and everyone on your left is 'team punch.'

If you shout 'kick,' team punch chase team kick to their wall. If anyone is caught by their partner, they do three burpees.

Progression - After a few turns, use Korean / Japanese terms instead. In our style of taekwondo this would be *jirugi* vs *chagi*.

BODYWEIGHT DRILLS

Not every drill requires kick pads, blockers or sparring kit. Here are ten simple but effective exercises that require no equipment.

Superman Bananas

Age range: All ages.

Goal: Core strength.

This is a quick drill that only requires thirty seconds. Have your students lay on their backs then raise their upper bodies and legs so only their bottom touches the floor. This is the banana position.

Everyone then needs to roll onto their belly but without letting their arms, chest or legs touch the floor. This is the Superman position.

Move between Superman and banana poses as many times as you can in the time allowed.

Bottom Balance Wars

Age range: All ages.

Goal: Core strength. Balance.

Sit facing a partner and lift your feet and hands off the floor. Align your feet with those of your partner and try to push each other off balance. If anything other than your bottom touches the floor do two burpees before finding a new partner and trying again.

Sumo Balance Wars

Age range: All ages.

Goal: Core and lower body strength. Balance.

Face a partner and sink down into a deep squat. Your bottom should be lower than your knees, preferably almost to the floor.

Palm to palm, try to push your partner off balance. If anything other than your feet touch the floor do two push-ups and find a new partner.

Plank Balance Wars

Age range: All ages.

Goal: Core strength. Balance.

Find a partner and face each other in a plank position. (Palms down rather than forearms). Try to pull your partner off balance by grabbing their wrist, pushing and pulling.

If you collapse out of your plank do ten star jumps and find a new partner.

TUNNELS

Age range: All ages.

Goal: Core and upper body strength. Teamwork.

Work in teams. Everyone forms a line and places their hands on the floor and pushes their middle as high as they can. The student at the end of the row army crawls through the human tunnel until they reach the end. They now become the front of the tunnel. Continue for a set amount of time or race against another team to see which tunnel can get to the other end of the dojo first.

Roll Over

Age range: +8.

Goal: Teamwork. Just for fun.

I used to hate this exercise when I was a self-conscious teenager. It involves a lot of body contact and as a forty-five kilo, fifteen-year-old girl I had no intention of joining in if I was in a team of sweaty, ninety-kilo grown men. (And quite rightly so!)

I still use this drill in my clubs today, it's a good giggle but it is strictly separated by age and gender and it is completely optional.

Get into teams and lie next to each other as close as possible. Don't leave any gaps. The student at the end of the team log rolls over the top of his or her teammates until they fall off the end of the row. Each player rolls in turn until the team makes it to the other end of the dojo.

King Of The Mats

Age range: +10.

Goal: Endurance, competitive spirit, tactics.

Designate a playing arena for your dojo. In my club, we have a wooden floor and lay mats on top. The mats are the arena and if you touch the wooden floor around it, you are out.

For this game, everyone finds a space and sits on their bottoms. When the game begins move around the arena in a crab like fashion (face up, hands on the floor behind you). The aim of the game is to push and pull other players until they are out of the arena.

You can wrestle, but no kicking or punching allowed.

You can sit, lie down, roll over... but you can not stand up.

Continue until only one person survives and is crowned King or Queen Of The Mats.

CRAB SPARRING

Age range: +10.

Goal: Endurance, competitive spirit, tactics. Teamwork.

This is a fun team game that requires tactics as well as strength.

Form two equal teams and choose a king for each team. Don't tell the other team who your king is.

The teams face each other and adopt a crab posture (facing up, hands on the floor behind you, bottom lifted off the floor).

The two teams move towards each other and try to push and pull other players off balance. If your bottom touches the floor you are out. Be careful! Once your king is out the team has lost.

Tactics involve protecting the king without letting the other team know who it is, ganging up on the other team's stronger players, and rushing to the help of teammates who are under attack.

HELICOPTERS

Age range: All ages.

Goal: Coordination, jumping skills.

This is another quick and easy exercise that only requires a couple of minutes but is sure to get the heart and lungs going.

Grab a partner. Student A sits on the floor with their legs stretched out in front of them as if about to do the sit and reach stretch. They then lift their arms to the side to shoulder height.

Student B jumps over their partner's legs, then jumps over the first arm, then crawls under the second arm to bring them back to where they started.

Student B performs three circles then swaps over. Complete as many sets as you can in the time allowed.

BURPEE LADDER

Age range: All ages.

Goal: Coordination, leg strength.

In pairs, have Student A drop down into a burpee. When Student A is in the lowest part of the burpee (the plank position) have Student B jump over them and drop into a burpee of their own. At this point Student A should be back up and jumping over Student B.

Move all the way down then dojo jumping over each other's burpees.

TAEKWONDO: THE MUSICAL

Or Karate: The Musical, or Kick Boxing: The Musical. Whatever works for you. Playing music in class boosts energy levels and can allow some creativity if different exercises are allocated to different lyrics.

GHOSTBUSTERS

Age range: All ages.

Goal: Endurance, leg strength, listening skills.

Play *Ghostbusters* by Ray Parker Jr and have everyone stand in a circle and begin lunges. Lunge all the way through the song unless you hear these lyrics:

'Ghostbusters!' = Burpee (with or without a push-up)

'I ain't afraid of no ghost' = Sit-up.

SALLY

Age range: +10.

Goal: Endurance, perseverance, listening skills.

Play *Flower* by Moby and choose either the plank, squat or push-up version.

Sally Up Plank Challenge:

'Bring Sally up' = Move into the high plank

'Bring Sally down' = Move to the low plank.

Sally Up Squat Challenge:

'Bring Sally up' = Stand normally

'Bring Sally down' = Squat down and hold until told to come back up.

Sally Up Push-Up Challenge:

'*Bring Sally up*' = Hold the high plank.

'*Bring Sally down*' = Lower into your push-up and hold at the lowest point until told to come back up.'

Can you make it to the end? It might only be thirty push-ups but those holds are a killer!

Cups

Age range: +10.

Goal: Endurance, core strength, listening skills.

Play *Cups* by Anna Kendrick and get into a plank.

On every *'when I'm gone'* do a push-up and on every *'you're gonna miss me'* do a sit-up. It sounds simple but it gets pretty fast in places and you have to roll back and forth between sit-ups and push-ups in time for the next lyric.

CHA CHA SLIDE

Age range: +10.

Goal: Endurance, core strength, listening skills. Memory.

This one is lots of fun and there are plenty of commands to memorise. Play *Cha Cha Slide* by DJ Casper and get into a plank position. Hold the plank unless told otherwise.

'Everyone clap your hands' = Shoulder taps.

'To the right / left' = Move your plank one step to the side.

'Take it back' = Move you plank backwards by one step.

'One hop this time' = One bunny hop.

'Two hops this time' = Two bunny hops.

'Five hops this time' = Five bunny hops.

'*Right / left foot let's stomp*' = Stomp your foot out to the side.

'*Right / left foot two stomps*' = Stomp your foot twice to the side.

'*Crisscross*' = Cross your feet over each other then return to normal.

'*Cha Cha real smooth*' = Eight mountain climbers.

'*Hands on your knees*' = Alternate tapping your left hand to your right knee and your right hand to your left knee.

'*Freeze! Everybody clap your hands*' = Freeze, then clap your hands because the workout is over!

Three Lions

Age range: All ages.

Goal: Endurance, upper and lower body strength, listening skills.

We got into the spirit of the Fifa World Cup by devising a workout to *Three Lions* by The Lightning Seeds. Everyone enjoyed singing along while they worked out. Not English? No problem. Choose any repetitive song that represents your country and add your own exercises to the lyrics. Making it up is half the fun.

Jog on the spot, pretend to dribble or head a football unless you hear these lyrics:

'It's coming' = Squat

'Three Lions' = Three push-ups

'England' = Burpee

'And Nobby dancing' = Do a little dance!

HAPPY HOLIDAYS

Around Christmas time we get very creative and invent all sorts of fun themes for the class. Here I share five of my favourites.

The 12 Days of Kickmas

Age range: +10.

Goal: Endurance, technique repetition, lower body strength and endurance.

This involves a whopping 364 kicks. You'll need a partner and a kick shield.

This works just like the song. In round one you perform one kick, then in round two you perform two kicks, plus the kick from round one. In round three you have three kicks, plus the two kicks from round two and kick from round one. And so on and so on...

"On the 1st day of kickmas the black belts made me do a jumping front snap kick."

"On the second day of kickmas the black belts made me do; two switch kicks and a jumping front snap kick."

"On the third day of kickmas the black belts made me do; three pushing kicks, two switch kicks and a jumping front snap kick."

4 = Four side kicks

5 = Hooking kick

6 = Back kicks

7 = Spin kicks

8 = Knee strikes

9 = Round kicks

10 = Axe kicks

11 = Jumping back kicks

12 = Tornado kicks

ADVENT CALENDAR

Age range: All ages.

Goal: Just for fun.

Make your own advent calendar by printing a grid with different exercises in each square. Then cover each square with a numbered Post-It note.

Choose a student to come out from the class and open a door (can be any door, doesn't have to be in order). They peel off the Post-It and read to the class what everyone will be doing. Continue until you run out of time or run out of doors.

Examples:

5 push-ups

50 star jumps

10 laps of the dojo

5 rounds of sparring

3 katas

Pull a silly face

Tell the person next to you a joke

Plank for one minute

Last Class Of The Year

Age range: +10.

Goal: Endurance, technique repetition, upper body strength and endurance.

We've done this for a number of years now and it's a great way to end the year on a high.

In the last class of 2017, we completed 2017 punches. In a forty-five minute class, that means almost forty-five punches per minute, every minute!

We fit it all in by using a mix of shadow sparring and bag work.

First Class of the Year

Age range: +10.

Goal: Endurance, technique repetition, lower body strength and endurance.

We can guess where this one is heading! Yes, the first class of 2018 involved 2018 kicks. This is such hard work and should probably be saved for your advanced teenagers. It is guaranteed to tire out even the strongest of legs.

Use a mixture of bag work and shadow work to fit all the reps in.

THE NICE LIST & THE NAUGHTY LIST

Age range: +10.

Goal: Coaching skills, teamwork, technique repetition.

For this class, I write two lesson plans and hide them in separate folders. I explain to the group that one folder contains The Nice List (basically my dream lesson plan including all the exercises and combinations I love to do; core work, switch kicks, axe kicks, lunges) and that the other folder contains The Naughty List (all the exercise and combos I'm not so fond of; push-ups, back kicks, hook kicks, burpees).

The students then find a partner and decide without looking in the folder if they want to be on the Naughty List or the Nice List.

It's fun watching my students try to guess what is in each plan. 'We should do the nice list. I bet it's full of side kicks and superman punches.'

'No, we should do the naughty list, I bet it's full of jumping kicks and push-ups.'

Once they choose they cannot switch back! Then basically, sit back and relax. Your class will teach itself.

10 MORE GAMES

The Ninjas Are Coming

Age range: -8.

Goal: Teamwork, technique repetition.

This is a quick game for your younger students. Choose a technique (something simple like sitting stance middle punch) Have the group run or shadow spar around the dojo. When you shout 'THE NINJAS ARE COMING!!' they shout back 'HOW MANY?'

If you shout 'THREE' everyone should get into threes and form sitting stance middle punches.

The winning team is the first group to form a three and stand in the correct technique.

Option 1 - To make this drill harder, you can say the name of the technique but not demonstrate it to the group.

Option 2 - To make this really hard, say the technique in Korean / Japanese terminology if this applies to your style.

THE OPPOSITE GAME

Age range: All ages.

Goal: Concentration, coordination, reaction speed.

In the opposite game, everything is backwards. If you shout 'STOP' everyone begins to run, and if you shout 'GO' everyone freezes.

To add a martial arts spin to this game we have some extras to add in:

'Punch' = Kick

'Kick' = Punch

'Low block' = High block

'High block' = Low block

'Up' = lie down

'Down' = tuck jump

Once you start shouting the commands in quick succession the game becomes very confusing. If your club is anything like mine, the children will ace this game and the adults will find it very confusing.

Creeping Lions

Age range: -8.

Goal: Technique repetition, concentration.

Have all your students stand in a row at the back of the dojo and choose a technique. In this example, we'll use walking stance middle block.

Turn your back on your students and have them creep forwards. When you turn around they must freeze in walking stance middle block.

You can send them back to the start line for two reasons:

1. You see them move.
2. You need to correct their technique.

Turn your back again and repeat until someone manages to make it all the way to the other end of the hall.

Emphasise that you can not win the game if you don't concentrate on technique.

General Choi Went to the Dojo

Age range: All ages.

Goal: Technique repetition, memory skills. Allow students to contribute to the class.

This is a memory game that includes technique repetition. I let students who are concentrating on their technique rather than rushing choose the different techniques to include.

We start by choosing a stance, let's say sitting stance, and a technique, let's say middle punch.

'General Choi went to the dojo and practiced sitting stance middle punches'... everyone practices the technique five times.

Choose the next student and have them add on a move to make a combination. 'General Choi went to the dojo and practiced sitting stance middle punch, rising block'... everyone performs middle punch, rising block five times.

You can keep playing as long as you like, making the combination longer and longer.

If you don't practice taekwondo you can change the name and set up of the exercise to suit your own style...

'Bruce Lee went to the dojo and practiced...'

'Kung Fu Panda went to the dojo and practiced...'

Higher or Lower

Age range: All ages.

Goal: Just for fun.

Use a random card generator app or bring a set of playing cards to class. Display the first card then ask the first student in line if the next card will be higher or lower.

Reveal the next card. If they are correct they move to the back of the queue. If they are wrong they perform a penalty such as ten star jumps.

PROVE IT

Age range: +8.

Goal: Just for fun. Technique repetition. Speed and endurance.

My students love this game. Have everyone sit in a circle and ask an assistant to hold a kick shield.

Start the game by saying something which is obviously true, such as 'I can do ten punches in thirty seconds.'

The student to your left has to either say a higher number ('I can do twenty-five punches in thirty seconds') or they tell you to prove it.

Continue around the circle with the number increasing higher and higher.

'I can do ninety-eight punches in thirty seconds!'

'PROVE IT!' shouts the next in line.

The student who claimed they could do ninety-eight punches approaches the kick shield, the timer is set and off he goes.

If he can do the number he said, the student who called him out has to perform a penalty. We use one hundred mountain climbers. If he can't do it, the puncher has a different penalty.

Try this game with how many kicks you can do in thirty seconds, or how many kicks you can do without putting your foot down.

Taekwondo Master

Age range: All ages.

Goal: Technique repetition, leadership skills. Just for fun.

Choose a student to be the detective. They hide in the corner and cover their eyes.

The rest of the group form a circle and the instructor selects a student to be the Taekwondo Master. Everyone in the group copies the Taekwondo Master as he changes between punches, kicks, star jumps etc.

The detective takes his place in the centre of the circle and tries to work out who everyone is copying. He has three guesses.

The Shuffle Game

Age range: All ages.

Goal: Just for fun. Core strength.

Have all you students sit with their hands on their heads at the far end of the training hall. Choose a handful of students to stand up.

Everyone who is sitting down begins to wiggle their way across the dojo. Their bottoms must stay on the floor and their hands must stay on their heads.

The students who are standing up have to try to stop their classmates from reaching the other end of the room. They can grab students by the back of the belt and drag them back to where they started. If someone isn't wearing a belt you can grab under their arms instead.

Ninja Jumps

Age range: -8.

Goal: Coordination, jumping skills, balance.

Your students find a space and begin to bounce up and down in a guarding stance as if about to spar.

On the command 'NINJA JUMP', everyone jumps as high as they can and switches stance. Encourage your students to tuck their knees up as they jump.

On the command 'NINJA DOUBLE JUMP', everyone jumps as high as they can and switches stance twice.

On the command 'SUPER NINJA JUMP', everyone jumps in the air and spins 360°, landing back where they started.

Option - We kiap on ninja jumps and ninja double jumps which means it gets super loud. On super ninja jump we go 'weeeeee'.

Ninja Statues

Age range: -8.

Goal: Technique repetition. Just for fun.

Everyone shadow spars in a space. When you shout 'NINJA STATUES' they should freeze in their favourite technique.

Have them hold the technique for a few seconds while you point out any great choices, correct any technique etc. Repeat five or six times, each time everyone needs to choose a different technique to freeze in.

THE FINAL FAVOURITE - DRILL 101

Bully It, Save It

Age range: +10.

Goal: Upper body endurance, competitive spirit.

A new addition to our repertoire of drills but an instant hit with young and old alike.

For this drill, you need a partner of similar strength (males and females separate) and a kick shield.

Lay the kick shield on the floor and decide who will attack and who will defend.

The rules are simple; Student A's job is to defend the kick shield from Student B.

Student B has to punch the shield as much as possible in one minute. Student A tries to stop them.

You can not hit each other but you can wrestle, push, pull, generally get in the way. You can not pick up the shield and run off with it but you can slide or push it along the ground.

SO LONG, FAREWELL

Phew. We did it! We got through all one hundred and one games, drills and exercises. Well done, everyone.

I hope you have as much fun using these games and drills in your classes as I do in mine.

If you enjoyed this book please get in touch. I'd love to know which drills your students couldn't get enough of and which drills got everyone red-faced and out of breath.

Twitter - @NE_MartialArts

Please consider taking a few minutes out of your day to rate this book and leave a review. I would greatly appreciate it.

Happy kicking,

Faye

Printed in Dunstable, United Kingdom